FAMOUS PEOPLE
FAMOUS LIVES

Biographies of famous people to
support the curriculum.

George
Stephenson

by Emma Fischel
Illustrations by Lynne Willey

W
FRANKLIN WATTS
LONDON•SYDNEY

First published in 2000 by
Franklin Watts
96 Leonard Street
London
EC2A 4XD

Franklin Watts Australia
56 O'Riordan Street
Alexandria
NSW 2015

ISBN: 0 7496 3682 3

Dewey Decimal Classification Number: 621.1

A CIP catalogue record for this book
is available from the British Library.

Series editor: Sarah Ridley
Historical consultant: Barbara Searle

Printed in Great Britain

George Stephenson

Little George was born into a very poor family. He didn't learn to read or write, and he didn't go to school.

But he DID ask a lot of questions.

George's father worked in a mine, where coal was dug out from deep under the ground. Sometimes George went with him to the mine.

He asked lots of questions there too.

Then he went home and built
models of things he had seen in
the mine.

A mine closed as soon as no more coal could be found underground.

Each time that happened, all the workers had to find jobs in other mines – and that meant moving house.

Moving house was a very slow business in those days. There were no cars or planes, or even bicycles.

There were no trains, either ... until George grew up, that is.

DEWLEY BURN
MINE
WORKERS WANTED

When he was only eight, George took his first job, looking after cows. Two years later he was working in the mine.

He worked on lots of different machines. If they went wrong he took them to bits, saw how they worked,

and put them right.

The bosses soon noticed George. They gave him more and more important jobs.

By the time he was seventeen George was his father's boss!

When George's father was a boy not many machines had been invented. But by the time George was growing up that was changing fast. Clever people were building new machines all over the country.

"I'm sure I can invent machines too," George said. "But first I need to learn about the ones already built."

And THAT was a problem because George couldn't read.

1769

My very important steam engine makes lots of other machines work.

JAMES WATT

11

"Night school," said George. "That's where I'll go."

George was eighteen now. He worked in the mine all day then studied at night.

"Your spelling and writing are awful," said his teacher. "But you're brilliant at sums!"

By the time he was twenty-two
George was married and had a
baby son, Robert.

Baby Robert didn't stop him
studying or trying to think of
ideas for machines...

LITTLE PUSHES TO
WHEEL, SEND IT ON AND
ON, SO WORKS FOREVER

MACHINES

SEED DRILL (JETHRO TULL)

but he did slow George down
a little.

The next few years didn't go
well. George's wife, Fanny, died.
Then his father was blinded in
an accident and couldn't work
any more. He had no money.

So George had to work harder
than ever.

Sometimes he despaired.

"How can I ever make a better life for us?" he said. "I must learn more. I must think up new machines. But there's no time."

His luck was about to change, though.

"Our brand new machine has gone wrong," said George's bosses. "And no one can fix it. You have a go, but don't take it to bits!"

No one thought George would
get it to work. George wasn't sure
he would either. For three days
and nights he hardly ate or slept.

At last he was ready.
"Start the engine!" he said.

It worked! "Brilliant!" said the bosses. "Have this better job with more money!"

Now George could pay for Robert to go to school. And what Robert learnt by day ...

George learnt by night.

George was working on a very big idea, too. The new machines all used lots of coal. He wanted to find cheaper and faster ways to get coal from the mines to the factories.

George went to his bosses. "Let me build a locomotive!" he said.

"A loco-what?" they said.

"A travelling engine that goes along rails!" said George. "A machine that can move on its own and pull heavy things behind it!"

Strange idea. No faster than horses.

Costs too much and it won't last long.

There will be accidents.

George wasn't the first to think of the idea ...

but he planned to be the best.

"We've never built a locomotive before," said the people George chose to help him.

"Nor have I!" said George.

"Will my first locomotive ever be finished?" wondered George.

It was in the end – and it worked!

"Bravo!" said everyone.

"Not good enough," said George. "Take it to bits! Change the wheels! Change the engine! Change everything!"

George was thirty-three now.
For the next ten years he worked
on building better locomotives.

Then he had another very
important idea.

"Good locomotives can't run on
bad rails," he said. "Change the
shape and the length! Change
how they fit together, and make
them of metal, not wood!"

HETTON COLLIERY LINE
BUILT BY GEORGE STEPHENSON
8 MILES LONG
FOR TAKING COAL FROM MINE
TO RIVERBOATS

A lot of ordinary people thought railways were a crazy idea.

So did important people in Parliament.

But one man, Edward Pease, had plans for a new kind of railway line, a much longer one between two towns.

He nagged members of Parliament again and again.

"Go ahead," they said in the end. "And please go away!"

"Build the new line," said Edward to George. "You're the only one who can!"

But other important businessmen didn't think locomotives would work on long trips. George had something to say about *that*.

Locomotives are the future and your ideas are the past!

Then Edward helped George open a factory with Robert, who was now grown up.

"You make the locomotives while I build the line," said George to Robert. "With your education and my ideas, together we're a team!"

George set to work on building
the first ever proper railway line.
No one could help him because
no one had done it before.

There were no huge machines to
help, either. George and his
team had buckets and shovels
and a few simple tools.

Day in, day out, they dug huge
chunks out of the earth and laid
the great tracks down.

The work was hard and
dangerous – and no one worked
harder than George. He was first
to arrive each morning and last
to leave each night.

"The track is ready!" said George at last.

"And so is Locomotion Number 1!" said Robert.

The first train was about to run on the first proper railway line in the world !

People flocked to watch in their thousands. Most of them had never even seen a train before.

With a great hiss of steam and a roaring cheer from the crowd Locomotion set off on its first great journey.

"I'm forty five, I'm rich, I'm famous – and locomotives are here to stay," said George. "My worries are over!"

But when a group of businessmen asked George to build a railway between Liverpool and Manchester, he ran into trouble again.

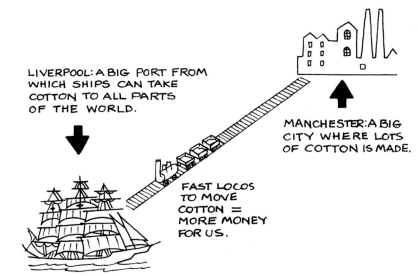

LIVERPOOL: A BIG PORT FROM WHICH SHIPS CAN TAKE COTTON TO ALL PARTS OF THE WORLD.

MANCHESTER: A BIG CITY WHERE LOTS OF COTTON IS MADE.

FAST LOCOS TO MOVE COTTON = MORE MONEY FOR US.

This railway line was fought against even harder than the first!

A lot of the early work had to be done in secret at night. They even hired a boxer to protect the workers from angry protesters.

At last George was allowed to start work on the line.

"He'll never build it. It's too hard," many people said. "And one bit is impossible!"

"I'll do the impossible bit first," said George.

After that he sorted out the rest.

"I can build a railway line anywhere," George said. "Who knows, one day locomotives may travel to towns all over the country!"

But the owners of *this* line weren't sure about locomotives either.

"We'll have a competition," they said. "That'll show us if these machines are any good *and* who can build them best!"

"We're going to build a brand-new locomotive, the best ever," said George. "We'll call it the Rocket, and we'll win!"

And while George was busy building the line, Robert built George's new locomotive – or tried to.

Five locomotives were ready on the day and thousands of people gathered to watch them.

Two days of tests went by, and no one could tell which was best.

Then the judges made the tests much, much harder. For three more days the locomotives steamed up and down the railway line. One after another they broke down – except for the Rocket.

George and Robert had done it!

And so the new Liverpool to
Manchester line opened, built
by George and running his
locomotives. It was a huge
success from the start.

"George Stephenson is the greatest railway engineer in the world," everyone said. Now there was no doubt – locomotives were here to stay!

George was forty-eight now. He spent the next twenty years helping to plan and build lots of new railways all over Britain.

He went to other countries too.

He built more locomotives, and never stopped trying to think of ways to make them better.

He was sixty-seven when he died. By then people could travel all over the country by train – just like George had always said they would.

Further facts

Safety lamp

In 1815 George developed a miner's
safety lamp. This lamp changed
colour when there was a poisonous
gas in the air and so saved miners'
lives. Sir Humphry Davy designed an
almost identical lamp at the same
time. He won the
£2,000 prize for
his lamp and
called George a
thief for stealing
his idea. Lots of
people thought
that George should

have got the prize and they raised
£1,000 for him.

Reading and writing

George could never read and write all that well. Even when he became rich and famous, he got other people to read or write for him whenever he could. And he never learnt to spell properly either!

Museums

The Rocket is the most famous locomotive ever built. You can see it in the Science Museum in London, along with Locomotion, George's first proper railway locomotive. Other early trains, such as the trains used by the royal family, can be seen at the Railway Museum in York.

Some important dates in George Stephenson's lifetime

1781 George is born in Wylam, near Newcastle.

1802 George marries Fanny Henderson.

1803 George's son, Robert, is born.

1812 George mends the Killingworth engine.

1814 George's first locomotive, Blücher, runs at Killingworth.

1823 George starts to build the Stockton to Darlington railway line. It opens in 1825.

1826 George starts work on the Liverpool to Manchester railway line.

1829 The Rocket wins the Rainhill Trials.

1830 The Liverpool to Manchester Railway opens.

1848 George dies at home in Tapton House, Chesterfield.